Table of Contents

Chapter 1: Introduction to Cardano 3
- What is Cardano? 3
- The Importance of ADA 4
- Overview of the Cardano Ecosystem 5
- Blockchain Basics 7
- The Ouroboros Protocol 8
- Key Components of Cardano 9

Chapter 3: Cardano Smart Contracts 12
- Introduction to Smart Contracts 12
- Developing Smart Contracts on Cardano 13
- Use Cases for Smart Contracts 14

Chapter 4: The Role of Proof of Stake 16
- Understanding Proof of Stake 16
- How Cardano Implements Proof of Stake 17
- Benefits of Proof of Stake for Cardano 18

Chapter 5: Decentralized Finance (DeFi) on Cardano 21
- What is DeFi? 21
- Key DeFi Applications on Cardano 22
- Future of DeFi in the Cardano Ecosystem 23

Chapter 6: Cardano Governance 25
- Introduction to Blockchain Governance 25
- Voting Mechanisms in Cardano 26
- Community Involvement and Decision Making 27

Chapter 7: Comparing Cardano with Other Blockchain Platforms 30
- Overview of Major Blockchain Platforms 30
- Strengths and Weaknesses of Cardano 31
- Unique Features of Cardano 32

Chapter 8: The Future of Cardano 35
- Roadmap Overview 35
- Upcoming Features and Enhancements 36
- Long-term Vision for Cardano 37

Chapter 9: Getting Started with Cardano 39
- Setting Up a Wallet 39
- Buying and Staking ADA 40
- Resources for Continued Learning 41

Chapter 1: Introduction to Cardano

What is Cardano?

Cardano is a multi-layered blockchain platform that was designed to provide a more secure and sustainable environment for the development of decentralized applications and smart contracts. Launched in 2017 by Charles Hoskinson, one of the co-founders of Ethereum, Cardano aims to address some of the challenges faced by earlier blockchain technologies, such as scalability, interoperability, and sustainability. The platform operates on a unique proof-of-stake consensus mechanism called Ouroboros, which is more energy-efficient than traditional proof-of-work systems, making it an attractive choice for developers and users alike.

At the core of Cardano is its native cryptocurrency, ADA, which serves as both a means of transaction and a tool for governance within the ecosystem. ADA holders can stake their tokens to support network operations and participate in the decision-making process regarding future upgrades and changes to the platform. This community-driven approach is a significant aspect of Cardano's philosophy, emphasizing transparency and inclusivity in its governance model. As more users engage with the platform, they contribute to its security and overall functionality while also earning rewards for their participation.

Cardano's architecture is divided into two primary layers: the Cardano Settlement Layer (CSL) and the Cardano Computation Layer (CCL). The CSL is responsible for handling transactions and maintaining the ledger of ADA, while the CCL manages smart contracts and decentralized applications. This separation allows for greater flexibility and scalability, as developers can deploy applications without compromising the security and efficiency of the underlying transaction layer. Such an arrangement is particularly beneficial for DeFi applications, which are increasingly gaining traction within the cryptocurrency space.

The introduction of smart contracts on Cardano has opened up a myriad of development opportunities, allowing developers to create decentralized applications that can operate in a wide range of industries.

From finance and supply chain management to healthcare and gaming, the potential use cases for Cardano's smart contracts are vast. Moreover, the platform's focus on formal verification ensures that these contracts are resilient and less prone to bugs or vulnerabilities, enhancing user trust and overall system integrity.

As Cardano continues to evolve, its roadmap includes various enhancements designed to expand its capabilities and user base. Upcoming features like improved interoperability with other blockchains and advanced governance mechanisms will further solidify its standing in the competitive blockchain landscape. By comparing Cardano with other platforms, it becomes evident that its unique combination of technological innovation and community involvement positions it as a strong contender for the future of decentralized finance and blockchain applications. Through continuous development and an engaged community, Cardano is poised to play a significant role in shaping the next generation of blockchain technologies.

The Importance of ADA

ADA, the native cryptocurrency of the Cardano blockchain, plays a crucial role in the ecosystem, serving various purposes that enhance the functionality and security of the network. At its core, ADA is used for transactions, enabling users to send and receive value in a decentralized manner. This feature is fundamental to any cryptocurrency, but what sets ADA apart is its integration within a robust proof-of-stake framework, which not only facilitates transactions but also encourages users to participate in network security and governance.

One of the most significant aspects of ADA is its role in the development and execution of smart contracts on the Cardano platform. As developers create decentralized applications (dApps), they rely on ADA to interact with these contracts. This integration ensures that transactions are executed smoothly and securely, allowing for a wide range of use cases, from simple token transfers to complex financial instruments. The ability to use ADA in smart contracts is essential for fostering innovation within the Cardano ecosystem, making it an attractive platform for developers and users alike.

In the context of decentralized finance (DeFi), ADA becomes even more critical. DeFi applications are transforming traditional financial systems by offering services such as lending, borrowing, and trading without intermediaries. ADA serves as a means of exchange, collateral, and governance within these applications. The growing interest in DeFi highlights the importance of ADA, as it enables users to access a new financial landscape that is more inclusive and accessible, aligning with Cardano's mission to empower individuals globally.

Governance is another vital area where ADA demonstrates its importance. Cardano employs a unique voting mechanism that allows ADA holders to participate in decision-making processes regarding the platform's future. This decentralized governance model ensures that the community has a voice in the development and direction of the ecosystem. By holding and staking ADA, users can contribute to proposals and influence changes, fostering a sense of ownership and collaboration within the Cardano community.

Finally, as Cardano continues to evolve, the roadmap for ADA includes upcoming features and enhancements that will further solidify its importance in the cryptocurrency landscape. Innovations such as improved scalability, interoperability with other blockchains, and enhanced user experience are all on the horizon. These developments not only promise to increase the utility of ADA but also position Cardano as a leading platform in the competitive blockchain space. Understanding the importance of ADA is essential for anyone looking to engage with Cardano and fully appreciate its potential in the rapidly changing world of cryptocurrency.

Overview of the Cardano Ecosystem

The Cardano ecosystem represents a comprehensive and innovative approach to blockchain technology, designed to provide a secure and scalable platform for the development of decentralized applications (dApps) and smart contracts. At its core, Cardano leverages a unique multi-layer architecture that separates the settlement layer, which handles the ADA cryptocurrency transactions, from the computation layer, where smart contracts are executed. This separation enhances the network's flexibility and scalability, allowing for upgrades and innovations without compromising the security of transactions.

A key feature of Cardano is its use of the Proof of Stake (PoS) consensus mechanism, called Ouroboros. Unlike traditional Proof of Work systems, which rely on energy-intensive mining processes, Ouroboros allows users to validate transactions and create new blocks based on the number of ADA tokens they hold and are willing to "stake." This not only makes Cardano more energy-efficient but also promotes greater participation from the community, as users can earn rewards for staking their tokens to help secure the network. The PoS system fosters a more inclusive environment, enabling individuals to contribute to the network's health without needing expensive hardware.

Smart contracts on Cardano open up a world of possibilities for developers and users alike. By utilizing the Plutus platform, Cardano provides a robust environment for creating and deploying smart contracts, facilitating various applications such as decentralized finance (DeFi) services, supply chain management, and identity verification. These smart contracts are designed to be secure and easily auditable, ensuring that users can trust the applications built on the Cardano blockchain. The growing ecosystem of dApps continues to attract developers looking for a reliable and efficient platform for their projects.

Decentralized finance (DeFi) is one of the most exciting components of the Cardano ecosystem. With DeFi applications, users can engage in activities such as lending, borrowing, and trading without relying on traditional financial institutions. Cardano's unique features, along with its strong focus on security and scalability, position it as a formidable player in the DeFi space. The community-driven approach to development allows for a diverse range of financial products and services, catering to a wide audience and fostering financial inclusivity.

Governance plays a crucial role in the Cardano ecosystem, empowering users to participate in decision-making processes that affect the network. The Cardano Improvement Proposal (CIP) process allows community members to propose changes or enhancements to the platform, ensuring that the development is in line with the collective vision of its users. This democratic approach to governance fosters a strong sense of community involvement, as ADA holders can vote on proposals and influence the future direction of the ecosystem. As Cardano continues to evolve, its commitment to community-driven governance will be essential in shaping its path forward.

Chapter 2: Understanding Cardano's Technology

Blockchain Basics

Blockchain technology serves as the foundational layer for cryptocurrencies, including Cardano and its native token, ADA. At its core, a blockchain is a decentralized and distributed digital ledger that records transactions across multiple computers. This structure ensures that the data is secure, transparent, and immutable, meaning once a transaction is recorded, it cannot be altered or deleted. Each block in the chain contains a number of transactions, and once filled, it is linked to the previous block, creating a chronological chain of data. This innovative design is pivotal in establishing trust among users without the need for a central authority.

Cardano stands out within the blockchain landscape due to its unique approach to scalability, security, and sustainability. It operates on a proof-of-stake consensus mechanism known as Ouroboros, which distinguishes it from traditional proof-of-work systems like Bitcoin. In proof-of-stake, validators are chosen to create new blocks based on the amount of ADA they hold and are willing to "stake" as collateral. This approach not only reduces energy consumption but also incentivizes users to participate in the network, promoting a more inclusive and environmentally friendly ecosystem.

Smart contracts are another critical component of blockchain technology, enabling automated and self-executing agreements without intermediaries. Cardano's smart contract functionality allows developers to build dApps (decentralized applications) that can be used in various sectors, from finance to healthcare. By leveraging the formal verification process, Cardano enhances the reliability and security of these contracts, making it a preferred platform for developers who prioritize safety and performance in their applications.

In the realm of decentralized finance (DeFi), Cardano is carving a niche that facilitates various financial services, such as lending, borrowing, and trading, all without traditional banking systems. DeFi applications on

Cardano leverage the blockchain's security and transparency, allowing users to engage in complex financial transactions directly on the network. This democratization of finance empowers individuals, giving them greater control over their assets and reducing reliance on centralized institutions.

Governance is another vital aspect of Cardano's ecosystem, enabling community involvement in decision-making processes. Through its innovative voting mechanisms, ADA holders can participate in shaping the future of the platform by voting on proposals and funding projects that align with their interests. This participatory approach fosters a sense of ownership and responsibility among users, ensuring that Cardano evolves according to the needs and desires of its community. As the platform continues to develop, understanding these blockchain basics will provide a solid foundation for navigating the exciting opportunities that lie ahead in the Cardano ecosystem.

The Ouroboros Protocol

The Ouroboros Protocol is a fundamental component of the Cardano blockchain, serving as its unique consensus mechanism. Unlike traditional proof-of-work systems that rely on energy-intensive mining, Ouroboros employs a proof-of-stake approach. This means that validators, or stakeholders, are chosen to create new blocks based on the number of coins they hold and are willing to "stake" as collateral. This method significantly reduces the energy consumption associated with blockchain operations and enhances the overall efficiency of the network. Understanding this protocol is crucial for anyone looking to navigate the Cardano ecosystem.

In the context of smart contracts, the Ouroboros Protocol plays a vital role in ensuring secure and efficient transactions. Smart contracts on Cardano are enabled through the use of the Extended UTXO (EUTXO) model, which allows for more complex computations and interactions. The Ouroboros mechanism ensures that these contracts are executed in a decentralized manner, maintaining the integrity and security of the transactions. As a beginner, grasping how Ouroboros interacts with smart contracts will provide insights into the practical applications of Cardano and how they differentiate it from other platforms.

The role of proof of stake via the Ouroboros Protocol extends beyond just securing the network. It fosters a more engaged community by allowing ADA holders to participate in the governance of the blockchain. Stakeholders can delegate their stakes to pools, supporting decentralized validation while also having a say in protocol upgrades and changes. This system of governance encourages community involvement and ensures that the development of Cardano aligns with the interests of its users. Newcomers should appreciate how this democratic approach empowers them in the ecosystem.

Cardano's focus on decentralized finance (DeFi) applications is also supported by the Ouroboros Protocol. The efficiency and security provided by this consensus mechanism facilitate the development of DeFi projects, which aim to replicate traditional financial services in a decentralized manner. With the ability to stake ADA and earn rewards, users can engage with various DeFi applications that are emerging within the Cardano ecosystem. Understanding the interplay between Ouroboros and DeFi is essential for those looking to explore investment opportunities and innovative financial products.

Looking ahead, the future of Cardano is closely tied to the ongoing enhancements of the Ouroboros Protocol. As the platform continues to evolve, new features and upgrades are expected to further improve scalability, interoperability, and user experience. Keeping abreast of these developments will be essential for anyone interested in Cardano. The roadmap for Cardano outlines ambitious plans that will build upon the strong foundation laid by the Ouroboros Protocol, promising a robust and dynamic ecosystem for both new and seasoned crypto enthusiasts.

Key Components of Cardano

Cardano is a complex yet fascinating blockchain platform distinguished by its innovative architecture and thoughtful design. Its key components include the Cardano blockchain itself, the native cryptocurrency ADA, the Ouroboros proof-of-stake consensus mechanism, and the multi-layer architecture that separates the settlement and computation layers. Each of these components plays a crucial role in the overall functionality and effectiveness of the Cardano ecosystem, making it a compelling option for both developers and users alike.

The Cardano blockchain serves as the foundation of the ecosystem, enabling secure and efficient transactions. Built with a modular design, it allows for flexibility and scalability, accommodating future upgrades and innovations without compromising the network's integrity. This adaptability is essential as the demand for blockchain technology continues to grow, particularly in areas like decentralized finance (DeFi) and smart contracts. The blockchain's robust security features protect against potential attacks and ensure the reliability of applications built on its platform.

At the heart of Cardano's operations lies ADA, the native cryptocurrency used for transactions and as a staking asset. ADA holders can participate in the network's proof-of-stake mechanism, which not only allows them to earn rewards but also empowers them to take part in the governance of the platform. This dual function of ADA highlights its significance, as it fosters community engagement and incentivizes users to contribute to the network's security and development. As more people become interested in Cardano, ADA's role as a utility token will likely expand, further enhancing its value proposition.

The Ouroboros consensus mechanism is another vital component of Cardano, distinguishing it from many other blockchain platforms that rely on energy-intensive proof-of-work systems. Ouroboros is designed to be energy-efficient while maintaining high levels of security and decentralization. It achieves this through a system of epochs and slots, where users can stake their ADA to create and validate blocks. This method not only reduces the environmental impact associated with blockchain operations but also aligns the interests of validators and stakeholders, promoting a more sustainable ecosystem.

The multi-layer architecture of Cardano separates its settlement layer, which handles transactions and ADA transfers, from its computation layer, responsible for executing smart contracts and decentralized applications. This separation is crucial for scalability and flexibility, allowing developers to create complex applications without compromising the network's performance. Moreover, Cardano's governance model encourages community involvement in decision-making processes, ensuring that the platform evolves according to the needs and aspirations of its users. As the ecosystem matures, these key components will play a pivotal role in shaping the future of Cardano and its position in the broader blockchain landscape.

Chapter 3: Cardano Smart Contracts

Introduction to Smart Contracts

Smart contracts are a pivotal innovation in the world of blockchain technology, representing self-executing agreements where the terms of the contract are directly written into code. These digital contracts automatically enforce and execute the terms when predefined conditions are met, eliminating the need for intermediaries. In the context of Cardano, smart contracts enhance the platform's capability to support decentralized applications (dApps) and facilitate complex financial transactions, making it a significant player in the evolving landscape of decentralized finance (DeFi).

Cardano's approach to smart contracts is characterized by its focus on security and scalability. The platform employs a unique programming language called Plutus, designed specifically for writing smart contracts. Plutus allows developers to create safe and reliable contracts by enabling formal verification, a method that mathematically proves the correctness of the code before deployment. This emphasis on security is crucial for gaining user trust and ensuring that applications built on Cardano can operate without vulnerabilities that could lead to financial loss or exploitation.

The introduction of smart contracts on Cardano has opened up numerous use cases across various industries. In finance, they can automate lending processes, create decentralized exchanges, and facilitate yield farming, allowing users to earn rewards on their crypto holdings. Beyond finance, smart contracts can revolutionize sectors such as supply chain management, gaming, and identity verification, providing transparency and efficiency in operations. As more developers and businesses recognize the potential of Cardano's smart contracts, the ecosystem is expected to expand significantly, attracting diverse projects and users.

Understanding the role of proof of stake (PoS) in Cardano's ecosystem is essential when discussing smart contracts. PoS not only enhances the security and sustainability of the network but also supports the execution of smart contracts by ensuring that the system remains decentralized and resilient against attacks. By using a PoS mechanism, Cardano allows users to participate in the network's governance and decision-making processes, fostering a community-driven approach that aligns with the principles of decentralization.

As Cardano continues to evolve, the integration of smart contracts marks a significant milestone in its roadmap. Future developments are aimed at improving the user experience, expanding the capabilities of dApps, and enhancing governance mechanisms. By comparing Cardano's smart contracts with those of other blockchain platforms, one can appreciate its unique features and advantages. The ongoing advancements in Cardano's ecosystem are poised to position it as a leading platform for smart contracts, driving innovation and adoption in the blockchain space.

Developing Smart Contracts on Cardano

Developing smart contracts on Cardano involves a unique blend of innovation and accessibility, making it an attractive option for those new to the world of blockchain technology. Unlike many other blockchain platforms, Cardano utilizes a distinct programming language called Plutus, which is designed to be both powerful and user-friendly. This allows developers to create complex smart contracts while also ensuring that the code is easily readable and maintainable. For beginners, understanding the fundamentals of Plutus and how it integrates with Cardano's architecture is essential for diving into smart contract development.

Cardano's approach to smart contracts is built on its proof-of-stake consensus mechanism, known as Ouroboros. This not only enhances security and scalability but also allows for more energy-efficient operations compared to proof-of-work systems. For newcomers, this means that participating in the Cardano ecosystem is not only environmentally friendly but also reduces the barriers to entry for developers. By leveraging the strengths of proof-of-stake, Cardano provides a robust framework for executing smart contracts that can handle a variety of applications, from simple transactions to complex decentralized finance (DeFi) solutions.

One of the significant advantages of developing smart contracts on Cardano is the emphasis on formal verification. This process involves mathematically proving the correctness of the code before it is deployed, significantly reducing the chances of bugs and vulnerabilities in the smart contracts. For those just starting, this feature can be reassuring, as it enhances the reliability of applications built on the Cardano blockchain. Formal verification is particularly beneficial in the DeFi space, where the stakes are high, and the potential for loss due to coding errors can be substantial.

In addition to security and efficiency, Cardano's ecosystem is rich with resources designed to support new developers. The community is active and welcoming, providing ample opportunities for learning through forums, tutorials, and workshops. Moreover, the platform's documentation is extensive, offering straightforward guidance on how to get started with smart contract development. This supportive environment is crucial for crypto newbies, as it fosters a sense of belonging and encourages experimentation without the fear of failure.

Looking ahead, the future of smart contract development on Cardano appears promising. The platform is continuously evolving, with upcoming features that aim to enhance functionality and user experience. Initiatives focused on governance and community involvement will likely play a significant role in shaping the direction of smart contracts within the ecosystem. As new tools and updates are released, developers will have even more opportunities to create innovative applications, making Cardano an exciting space for anyone looking to dive into the world of blockchain technology.

Use Cases for Smart Contracts

Smart contracts, self-executing contracts with the terms of the agreement directly written into code, represent a fundamental innovation within the blockchain space. On the Cardano platform, these contracts enable a range of applications that can automate processes and transactions without the need for intermediaries, enhancing efficiency and security. For crypto newbies, understanding the practical use cases of smart contracts can illuminate their potential and the transformative impact they can have across various industries.

One prominent use case of smart contracts on Cardano is in the realm of decentralized finance (DeFi). By enabling the creation of decentralized applications (dApps), Cardano allows users to lend, borrow, and trade assets without relying on traditional financial institutions. This not only democratizes access to financial services but also fosters an environment of trust, as transactions are executed transparently on the blockchain. Users can interact with various DeFi protocols without worrying about central authority interference, thus empowering individuals in their financial decisions.

Another significant application of smart contracts on Cardano is in supply chain management. By utilizing blockchain technology, companies can track the provenance of goods in real-time, ensuring transparency and accountability throughout the supply chain. Smart contracts can automate the verification of product authenticity and delivery conditions, reducing fraud and errors while improving efficiency. This level of traceability is particularly important in industries such as pharmaceuticals and food, where safety and quality assurance are paramount.

Moreover, smart contracts play a vital role in governance and voting mechanisms within the Cardano ecosystem. Through decentralized governance, stakeholders can propose and vote on changes or improvements to the network. Smart contracts facilitate this process by ensuring that votes are counted accurately and transparently, thereby fostering community involvement and democratic decision-making. This innovative approach to governance not only enhances user participation but also strengthens the overall resilience of the Cardano network.

Lastly, the integration of smart contracts can significantly impact real estate transactions. By automating agreements related to property sales and rentals, smart contracts can streamline processes such as title transfers and escrow services. This reduces the need for intermediaries like real estate agents and lawyers, resulting in lower transaction costs and faster closing times. As Cardano continues to evolve, the potential for smart contracts to revolutionize industries and improve everyday processes becomes increasingly evident, presenting exciting opportunities for both developers and users alike.

Chapter 4: The Role of Proof of Stake

Understanding Proof of Stake

Proof of Stake (PoS) is a consensus mechanism that plays a crucial role in the Cardano ecosystem, differentiating it from the more commonly known Proof of Work (PoW) model used by Bitcoin. In PoS, validators, or "stakers," are chosen to create new blocks and validate transactions based on the number of coins they hold and are willing to "stake" as collateral. This system incentivizes users to hold onto their ADA tokens, as the more they stake, the higher their chances of being selected to validate transactions and earn rewards. This not only secures the network but also reduces the energy consumption associated with mining, making PoS a more environmentally friendly option.

One of the key advantages of Proof of Stake is its efficiency in processing transactions. Unlike PoW, where miners compete to solve complex mathematical problems, PoS allows for a more streamlined process. Validators are selected in a pseudo-random manner, which means transactions can be confirmed more quickly and at a lower cost. This efficiency is particularly important for Cardano, as the platform aims to support a wide range of applications, including decentralized finance (DeFi) solutions and smart contracts, which require fast and reliable transaction processing.

Cardano's unique approach to PoS is embodied in its Ouroboros protocol, which is designed to ensure security and scalability. Ouroboros divides time into epochs and slots, allowing for a structured approach to block creation and validation. This design not only enhances the network's security by making it resistant to certain types of attacks but also allows Cardano to scale effectively as usage grows. As more users and applications interact with the Cardano blockchain, the PoS mechanism ensures that the network can adapt without sacrificing performance or security.

Another significant aspect of Proof of Stake in Cardano is its role in governance. Cardano encourages community participation through its staking model, where stakeholders have a say in governance decisions. This means that those who stake their ADA can vote on proposals that affect the future of the network, including updates and changes to protocol parameters. This democratic approach fosters a sense of community and ensures that the platform evolves in a way that reflects the interests of its users.

In summary, understanding Proof of Stake is essential for grasping how Cardano operates and what sets it apart from other blockchain platforms. Its efficient and eco-friendly consensus mechanism not only supports fast transaction processing but also integrates community governance into the decision-making process. As Cardano continues to grow and develop new features, the role of PoS will remain central to its mission of creating a sustainable and user-driven blockchain ecosystem. For newcomers to the world of crypto, grasping these concepts will provide a solid foundation for exploring Cardano's many offerings.

How Cardano Implements Proof of Stake

Cardano, a leading blockchain platform, employs a unique Proof of Stake (PoS) mechanism known as Ouroboros to validate transactions and secure its network. Unlike the traditional Proof of Work (PoW) systems used by Bitcoin, where miners compete to solve complex mathematical puzzles, Cardano's PoS allows participants, called stakeholders, to validate transactions based on the amount of cryptocurrency they hold and are willing to "stake." This approach not only enhances energy efficiency but also promotes decentralization by enabling a broader range of participants to contribute to network security and operations.

At the heart of Cardano's Proof of Stake model is the concept of epoch and slot. The blockchain is divided into epochs, which are further divided into slots. Each slot represents a specific period during which a block may be created. Stakeholders are assigned to validate transactions based on their stake and the random selection process governed by the Ouroboros protocol. This mechanism ensures that every stakeholder has a fair chance of being selected to produce a block, which fosters greater inclusivity and participation within the network.

Cardano's PoS system also incorporates a rewards mechanism that incentivizes stakeholders to participate actively. When a stakeholder is selected to create a new block, they receive rewards in the form of ADA, Cardano's native cryptocurrency. This reward system not only encourages users to stake their ADA but also aligns their interests with the network's health and security. The more ADA a user stakes, the higher their chances of being selected to validate transactions and earn rewards, creating a self-reinforcing cycle of participation and investment in the Cardano ecosystem.

Governance plays a pivotal role in Cardano's Proof of Stake framework. The platform empowers its community to participate in decision-making processes, allowing stakeholders to vote on protocol upgrades and changes. This democratic approach to governance ensures that the development of Cardano aligns with the interests and needs of its users. By leveraging the PoS model, Cardano promotes a sense of ownership and accountability among its community members, fostering a collaborative environment that drives innovation and growth within the ecosystem.

In summary, Cardano's implementation of Proof of Stake through the Ouroboros protocol marks a significant advancement in blockchain technology. By prioritizing energy efficiency, inclusivity, and community governance, Cardano not only enhances the security and scalability of its network but also sets a precedent for future blockchain projects. As the ecosystem continues to expand, understanding the intricacies of its PoS mechanism will be crucial for newcomers looking to navigate the world of Cardano and its myriad applications in decentralized finance and beyond.

Benefits of Proof of Stake for Cardano

Proof of Stake (PoS) offers several advantages for Cardano, distinguishing it from traditional Proof of Work (PoW) systems. One of the primary benefits is energy efficiency. PoW requires vast amounts of computational power to validate transactions, leading to high energy consumption. In contrast, Cardano's PoS mechanism allows validators to produce new blocks based on the number of coins they hold and are willing to "stake" as collateral. This significantly reduces energy requirements, promoting a more sustainable approach to blockchain technology, which is increasingly important in a world focused on environmental impact.

Another significant benefit of PoS in Cardano is enhanced security. In a PoS system, the likelihood of being chosen to validate the next block is proportional to the amount of cryptocurrency staked. This encourages holders to act honestly and maintain the network's integrity, as malicious actions could result in losing their staked assets. This built-in economic incentive helps deter attacks on the network, making Cardano more resilient to potential threats compared to networks relying on PoW, where attackers may find it easier to outpace honest miners.

Cardano's PoS model also fosters decentralization. By allowing a broader range of participants to become validators, the network can maintain a more distributed structure. In PoW systems, mining power tends to concentrate in the hands of a few entities with access to expensive hardware and cheap electricity. In Cardano, anyone with ADA can participate in the staking process, which empowers a larger segment of the community to contribute to the network's security and decision-making. This decentralization is vital for ensuring that no single entity can control the network, preserving its democratic nature.

Moreover, PoS incentivizes long-term investment in the Cardano ecosystem. When users stake their ADA, they not only help secure the network but also earn rewards for their participation. This creates a cycle where users are encouraged to hold onto their assets longer rather than engaging in short-term trading. As more ADA is staked, the overall network stability increases, contributing to higher transaction throughput and reliability. This long-term commitment can result in a more robust and healthy ecosystem, fostering innovation and development in various applications, including smart contracts and decentralized finance (DeFi).

Lastly, the governance model in Cardano is enhanced by the PoS mechanism. The network encourages active participation from its community members, allowing them to vote on proposals and changes to the protocol. This democratic approach ensures that users have a voice in the evolution of the Cardano ecosystem, making it more adaptable to the needs of its participants. By linking governance to staking, Cardano promotes an engaged and informed community that is invested in the platform's success, paving the way for continued growth and development in the blockchain space.

Chapter 5: Decentralized Finance (DeFi) on Cardano

What is DeFi?

Decentralized Finance, commonly known as DeFi, represents a transformative shift in the financial landscape by utilizing blockchain technology to recreate and improve traditional financial systems. Unlike conventional finance, which relies on centralized institutions such as banks and brokers, DeFi operates on decentralized networks, enabling direct peer-to-peer transactions. This framework eliminates intermediaries, thereby reducing costs and increasing accessibility for users. In essence, DeFi encompasses a wide range of financial services, including lending, borrowing, and trading, all facilitated through smart contracts on blockchain platforms.

Cardano, with its innovative proof-of-stake mechanism and robust smart contract capabilities, is well-positioned to contribute significantly to the DeFi movement. By leveraging the Cardano blockchain, developers can create decentralized applications (dApps) that facilitate various financial activities without the need for traditional banking infrastructure. These applications can range from decentralized exchanges to lending platforms and yield farming protocols, offering users the ability to engage in financial activities while maintaining control over their assets. The emphasis on security and scalability in Cardano's design further enhances its appeal to both developers and users in the DeFi space.

One of the key advantages of DeFi is its ability to enhance financial inclusivity. Traditional financial systems often exclude individuals without access to banking services or those in regions with underdeveloped financial infrastructure. DeFi democratizes access to financial tools, allowing anyone with an internet connection to participate in global financial markets. Cardano's approach to DeFi aims to bridge this gap by providing a user-friendly environment that supports a diverse range of financial services, thus empowering users from various backgrounds to engage in economic activities previously unavailable to them.

Moreover, DeFi fosters innovation by providing a platform for experimentation and development. Developers are encouraged to build novel financial instruments and services that can cater to specific needs and preferences, creating a dynamic ecosystem of financial products. Cardano's focus on formal verification and rigorous development processes ensures that these innovations are secure and reliable. As the DeFi landscape continues to evolve, Cardano's commitment to quality and safety positions it as a trustworthy foundation for new financial applications and services.

In summary, DeFi represents a paradigm shift in how financial services are structured and delivered, with Cardano emerging as a key player in this evolving space. The combination of decentralized infrastructure, enhanced accessibility, and innovative potential creates a fertile ground for new financial opportunities. As more users and developers engage with DeFi on the Cardano platform, the ecosystem is set to grow, offering a wide array of services that challenge traditional financial norms and empower individuals globally.

Key DeFi Applications on Cardano

Decentralized Finance, or DeFi, has gained immense traction in the cryptocurrency space, and Cardano is positioning itself as a strong contender in this evolving ecosystem. The platform's unique architecture, which includes a robust proof-of-stake consensus mechanism, allows for the efficient deployment of smart contracts and decentralized applications (dApps). This has paved the way for several key DeFi applications that leverage the capabilities of Cardano to provide innovative financial solutions. Understanding these applications is essential for anyone looking to explore the potential of Cardano and its impact on the broader financial landscape.

One of the most notable DeFi applications on Cardano is decentralized exchanges (DEXs). These platforms enable users to trade cryptocurrencies directly with one another without the need for a centralized intermediary. Cardano's DEXs harness the platform's scalability and low transaction costs to facilitate seamless trading experiences. By eliminating the middleman, users retain full control over their assets, enhancing security and reducing the risk of hacks and fraud, which are common in centralized exchanges.

Another significant application within the Cardano DeFi ecosystem is lending and borrowing platforms. These protocols allow users to lend their assets to others in exchange for interest, or to borrow funds by providing collateral. Cardano's smart contract capabilities enable the automation of these processes, ensuring transparency and trust. Users benefit from the ability to earn passive income on their holdings while simultaneously accessing liquidity without selling their assets. This creates a more dynamic financial environment where users can optimize their investments.

Yield farming and liquidity mining are also essential components of Cardano's DeFi landscape. These practices incentivize users to provide liquidity to DEXs or other financial products in exchange for rewards, typically in the form of tokens. Cardano's architecture supports these activities through efficient transaction processing and governance mechanisms that allow users to participate in decision-making regarding the protocol's future. This not only enhances user engagement but also fosters a sense of community ownership and responsibility.

Lastly, non-fungible tokens (NFTs) and tokenization of real-world assets are emerging as vital areas within Cardano's DeFi applications. By enabling the creation and trading of unique digital assets, Cardano offers opportunities for artists, creators, and investors alike. This intersection of DeFi and NFTs allows for innovative financial products and services, expanding the utility of the Cardano ecosystem. As these applications continue to evolve, they will play a crucial role in defining the future of finance on the Cardano platform, making it an exciting space for newcomers to explore.

Future of DeFi in the Cardano Ecosystem

The future of decentralized finance (DeFi) within the Cardano ecosystem looks promising as it continues to evolve and attract attention from developers and investors alike. Cardano's unique architecture, built on a proof-of-stake consensus mechanism, provides a solid foundation for DeFi applications. This system not only enhances security and scalability but also aligns with Cardano's commitment to sustainability. As more developers explore the capabilities of Cardano's smart contracts, we can expect a surge in innovative DeFi solutions that leverage the platform's strengths.

One of the key factors driving the future of DeFi on Cardano is the ongoing development of smart contracts. With the introduction of the Alonzo upgrade, Cardano has made it possible for developers to create complex financial applications that can operate seamlessly within its ecosystem. This development opens the door for projects that can provide lending, borrowing, and trading functionalities, similar to those found on other blockchain platforms. As the community continues to embrace these tools, we are likely to see an increase in user-friendly applications that democratize access to finance.

Interoperability is another critical component that will shape the future of DeFi on Cardano. The ability for Cardano to interact with other blockchains can enhance the functionality of its DeFi applications. This feature allows users to access a wider range of assets and services, creating a more interconnected financial environment. As Cardano develops bridges to other networks, the potential for cross-chain DeFi applications will grow, attracting a diverse user base and fostering collaboration within the broader blockchain ecosystem.

Governance also plays a vital role in the future of DeFi on Cardano. The platform's unique approach to community involvement through voting mechanisms empowers ADA holders to influence the direction of projects and initiatives. This democratic process encourages innovation, as developers are incentivized to create solutions that resonate with the community. As the governance model matures, it will likely lead to a more robust and responsive DeFi landscape that reflects the needs and desires of its users.

Looking forward, the roadmap for Cardano includes numerous upcoming features that will further enhance its DeFi capabilities. As the platform continues to roll out improvements and new tools, developers will have more resources at their disposal to create efficient and effective financial applications. This continuous development, coupled with an engaged community and a focus on interoperability, positions Cardano to become a significant player in the DeFi space. By staying informed and involved, newcomers to the Cardano ecosystem can participate in and benefit from the exciting advancements on the horizon.

Chapter 6: Cardano Governance

Introduction to Blockchain Governance

Blockchain governance is a critical aspect of decentralized networks, including Cardano, that ensures the system operates effectively and evolves in a way that meets the needs of its users. Unlike traditional governance structures, which typically rely on central authorities, blockchain governance emphasizes community involvement and consensus-driven decision-making. This decentralized approach empowers users to have a direct say in the development and direction of the platform, fostering a sense of ownership and accountability within the community.

At the heart of Cardano's governance model is the concept of decentralized decision-making, which allows stakeholders to participate actively in discussions and votes regarding protocol upgrades and changes. Cardano employs a unique system, where ADA holders can propose and vote on changes to the network through a structured process. This participatory model not only democratizes the governance process but also ensures that the interests of a diverse group of stakeholders are considered, enhancing the platform's resilience and adaptability.

One of the key components of Cardano's governance is its treasury system, which allocates funds for development and community projects. This system allows users to propose projects that can be funded through the treasury, creating an ecosystem where innovation is rewarded and supported. The treasury acts as a financial backbone for the community, enabling it to invest in improvements and new features that align with the collective vision of Cardano's future. This funding mechanism is essential for driving progress and ensuring that the ecosystem remains vibrant and responsive to user needs.

Voting mechanisms play a crucial role in Cardano's governance structure. Users can participate in governance through a process called Project Catalyst, which allows them to vote on funding proposals and contribute to the decision-making process. This platform not only empowers ADA holders but also encourages collaboration and discussion among community members. By actively engaging in governance, users can influence the direction of Cardano, making it a living, breathing ecosystem that evolves based on collective input and shared goals.

Understanding blockchain governance is essential for anyone looking to navigate the Cardano ecosystem effectively. As new developments and features are introduced, the role of governance will only become more prominent. For crypto newbies, grasping the principles of governance within Cardano will enhance their ability to participate meaningfully in discussions and decisions, paving the way for a more engaged and informed community. As Cardano continues to grow, the emphasis on a robust governance framework will be crucial for maintaining trust, transparency, and innovation in this dynamic digital landscape.

Voting Mechanisms in Cardano

Voting mechanisms in Cardano are a fundamental aspect of its governance model, allowing stakeholders to participate actively in decision-making processes that shape the future of the platform. At the core of Cardano's governance is the concept of decentralized decision-making, where ADA holders have the power to influence protocol upgrades, project funding, and other critical aspects of the ecosystem. This democratic approach not only fosters community engagement but also ensures that the platform evolves in a manner that reflects the interests of its users.

Cardano employs a unique voting system known as Project Catalyst, which serves as a framework for community-driven innovation. Through Project Catalyst, ADA holders can propose projects and initiatives aimed at enhancing the Cardano ecosystem. These proposals are subjected to a voting process where stakeholders can express their support or opposition. The outcome of these votes plays a significant role in determining which projects receive funding and resources, thereby facilitating a more vibrant and diverse ecosystem. This mechanism encourages creativity and collaboration among developers and community members alike.

The voting process in Cardano is designed to be straightforward and user-friendly. ADA holders participate in voting by using their wallets, where they can cast their votes on various proposals. The system ensures that each vote is weighted according to the amount of ADA held, promoting a fair representation of stakeholders' interests. This approach also aligns incentives, as participants are motivated to support proposals that will enhance the value of their holdings. By allowing stakeholders to have a direct say in the governance of the platform, Cardano fosters a sense of ownership and accountability among its community.

Security and transparency are paramount in Cardano's voting mechanisms. The entire process is built on blockchain technology, ensuring that all votes are recorded immutably and can be audited by any participant. This transparency helps to build trust within the community, as stakeholders can verify that the voting process is fair and tamper-proof. Additionally, Cardano's use of the Ouroboros proof-of-stake protocol enhances the security of the voting system, as it incentivizes honest participation and discourages malicious behavior.

As Cardano continues to evolve, its voting mechanisms are expected to adapt and improve. Ongoing developments aim to introduce more sophisticated features, such as enhanced voting interfaces and new ways to engage the community in governance. The future of Cardano's voting system looks promising, with the potential to further empower users and integrate their feedback into the platform's ongoing development. By prioritizing community involvement and transparent decision-making, Cardano sets a precedent for other blockchain projects seeking to create an inclusive and dynamic ecosystem.

Community Involvement and Decision Making

Community involvement is a cornerstone of the Cardano ecosystem, driving its development and governance. Unlike many traditional systems where decisions are made by a select few, Cardano embraces a decentralized approach, allowing all stakeholders to participate in the decision-making process. This democratic ethos is reflected in the platform's governance model, which emphasizes the importance of community input and collaboration. By actively engaging with the community, Cardano aims to create a more resilient and adaptable ecosystem that reflects the needs and desires of its users.

One of the key mechanisms for community involvement in Cardano is through its treasury system, which allocates funds for development projects based on community votes. Members of the Cardano community can propose initiatives that they believe will benefit the ecosystem. These proposals are then subjected to a voting process where ADA holders can express their opinions. The outcomes of these votes directly influence which projects receive funding, ensuring that the community has a tangible say in the future direction of Cardano. This process not only empowers users but also fosters a sense of ownership and responsibility among stakeholders.

In addition to voting on funding proposals, Cardano encourages community engagement through various forums and platforms. The Cardano Foundation, IOHK (Input Output Hong Kong), and Emurgo actively facilitate discussions and provide channels for feedback. These organizations host events, webinars, and workshops aimed at educating users about the platform and its features. By creating spaces for open dialogue, Cardano fosters a collaborative environment where ideas can flourish, and solutions to challenges can be collectively developed. This level of engagement is crucial for newcomers, as it helps them understand the intricacies of the ecosystem while also feeling valued as part of the community.

Cardano's governance model also incorporates innovative mechanisms such as Project Catalyst, which serves as an incubator for new ideas. This initiative allows community members to submit proposals for projects that can enhance the Cardano ecosystem. Not only does it provide funding for innovative ideas, but it also involves a robust feedback loop where the community can discuss and refine these proposals. This iterative process ensures that the projects receiving support align closely with the community's vision for Cardano's future. For crypto newbies, participating in Project Catalyst can serve as a practical entry point into understanding how governance and community involvement work in decentralized systems.

Ultimately, the strength of Cardano lies in its commitment to community-driven decision-making. As more users engage with the platform and participate in governance, Cardano's ability to adapt and evolve will be greatly enhanced. For those just beginning their journey into the world of Cardano, understanding the significance of community involvement is essential. It not only shapes the development of the ecosystem but also provides a unique opportunity for individuals to contribute to a project that prioritizes inclusivity and collaboration. By getting involved, new users can help define the trajectory of Cardano and ensure it remains a leading player in the blockchain landscape.

Chapter 7: Comparing Cardano with Other Blockchain Platforms

Overview of Major Blockchain Platforms

In the rapidly evolving world of blockchain technology, several platforms have emerged, each with unique features and functionalities. Understanding these major blockchain platforms is crucial for grasping the broader context in which Cardano (ADA) operates. This overview highlights key platforms that have influenced the industry, particularly in comparison to Cardano, which is known for its innovative approach to scalability, security, and sustainability through its proof-of-stake consensus mechanism.

Ethereum is one of the most prominent blockchain platforms, primarily recognized for its smart contract capabilities. Launched in 2015, Ethereum introduced a decentralized environment where developers could create and deploy decentralized applications (dApps). Its robust community and extensive developer support have made it the go-to platform for many DeFi projects. However, Ethereum's transition to a proof-of-stake model with Ethereum 2.0 aims to address scalability and energy consumption issues, making it a significant competitor to Cardano.

Another noteworthy platform is Binance Smart Chain (BSC), which has gained traction due to its low transaction fees and fast processing times. BSC has become a popular choice for dApps, particularly in the DeFi sector, as it allows users to trade and participate in yield farming with lower costs compared to Ethereum. While BSC offers a more centralized approach, relying on a smaller number of validators, it highlights the importance of user experience and accessibility, aspects that Cardano also prioritizes while maintaining a more decentralized framework.

Solana is another rising star in the blockchain ecosystem, known for its high throughput and low latency, which enables it to handle thousands of transactions per second. This capability makes Solana particularly appealing for applications requiring rapid processing, such as gaming and NFT marketplaces. However, its relatively young ecosystem and concerns over decentralization contrast with Cardano's emphasis on a methodical, research-driven approach to platform development. Cardano seeks to ensure long-term sustainability, making it a formidable player in the blockchain landscape.

Finally, Polkadot offers a unique perspective by allowing different blockchains to interoperate through its relay chain architecture. This multichain approach enhances scalability and enables various blockchains to communicate and share information. While Polkadot focuses on interoperability, Cardano's emphasis on formal verification and peer-reviewed research positions it as a reliable choice for developers seeking a secure and stable environment for their smart contracts and applications. Understanding these major blockchain platforms provides context for Cardano's innovations and its potential to shape the future of decentralized technology.

Strengths and Weaknesses of Cardano

Cardano, a prominent player in the blockchain realm, possesses distinct strengths that set it apart from its competitors. One of its most significant advantages lies in its proof-of-stake consensus mechanism, known as Ouroboros. This innovative approach not only promotes energy efficiency but also enhances scalability, allowing the network to process transactions more rapidly than traditional proof-of-work systems like Bitcoin. Furthermore, Cardano employs a rigorous academic and research-driven methodology for its development, ensuring that each upgrade and feature is backed by peer-reviewed studies. This foundation of academic rigor fosters a strong sense of trust and reliability within the community, attracting developers and investors alike.

Despite its notable strengths, Cardano also faces certain weaknesses that could impact its growth and adoption. One primary concern is its relatively slower pace of development compared to other blockchain platforms. While Cardano's commitment to thorough research and planning is commendable, it can lead to delays in the deployment of new features and functionalities. Additionally, the complexity of its architecture may pose challenges for new developers who are trying to navigate its ecosystem, potentially hindering the rate at which decentralized applications (dApps) are built on its platform.

Another aspect to consider is Cardano's governance model, which, while designed to be inclusive and democratic, can sometimes lead to indecision or fragmentation within the community. The voting mechanisms allow ADA holders to influence the direction of the project, which is a strength in terms of community involvement. However, this very inclusivity can also result in a lack of consensus during crucial decision-making processes, potentially slowing down crucial developments and implementations. Balancing community input with decisive leadership is a challenge that Cardano must address moving forward.

Moreover, the competitive landscape of blockchain technology presents ongoing challenges for Cardano. With numerous platforms vying for dominance in the DeFi space, Cardano must continuously innovate to maintain its relevance. Other blockchain networks, such as Ethereum, have established themselves firmly in the smart contract arena, making it imperative for Cardano to showcase unique use cases that highlight its advantages. The successful deployment of smart contracts on Cardano, particularly through its Alonzo upgrade, marks a critical step, but the platform must now demonstrate its capabilities through real-world applications to attract developers and users.

Looking to the future, Cardano's roadmap reveals a commitment to addressing its weaknesses while capitalizing on its strengths. Upcoming features aim to enhance user experience, improve scalability, and introduce new functionalities that can support a broader range of applications. By focusing on continuous development and community engagement, Cardano seeks to solidify its position in the blockchain ecosystem. For crypto newbies, understanding both the strengths and weaknesses of Cardano is essential for navigating its potential and making informed decisions about their involvement in this evolving digital landscape.

Unique Features of Cardano

Cardano is distinguished by several unique features that set it apart from other blockchain platforms, making it an appealing choice for both developers and users. One of the cornerstone attributes of Cardano is its innovative proof-of-stake consensus mechanism known as Ouroboros. Unlike traditional proof-of-work systems that require extensive computational power and energy consumption, Ouroboros allows ADA holders to participate in the network's security and transaction verification by staking their tokens. This not only enhances energy efficiency but also promotes a more inclusive approach to network participation, enabling a broader segment of the community to engage in governance and decision-making processes.

Another defining feature of Cardano is its layered architecture, which separates the settlement layer from the computation layer. This design allows for improved scalability and flexibility, as it enables smart contracts to be executed independently of the underlying cryptocurrency transactions. The settlement layer handles ADA transactions, while the computation layer is focused on running smart contracts and decentralized applications (dApps). This separation ensures that updates to the smart contract functionality can occur without disrupting the core financial transactions of the network, fostering a more stable and adaptable ecosystem.

Smart contracts on Cardano are developed using a unique programming language called Plutus, which is based on Haskell. This functional programming approach provides strong guarantees regarding the correctness and security of the code, reducing the risk of vulnerabilities that can lead to exploits or failures in decentralized applications. By offering a secure development environment, Cardano empowers developers to create robust dApps that can cater to various use cases, ranging from financial services to supply chain management. The emphasis on security and reliability makes Cardano an attractive option for enterprises looking to leverage blockchain technology.

In addition to its technical innovations, Cardano places a significant emphasis on governance and community involvement. The platform features a unique treasury system that allocates funds for future development based on community votes. This participatory governance model allows ADA holders to influence the direction of the network and its projects, fostering a sense of ownership and responsibility within the community. By prioritizing decentralization and user engagement,

Cardano aims to create a sustainable ecosystem where stakeholders have a voice in the platform's evolution.

Lastly, Cardano's commitment to research and development underpins its roadmap for the future. The platform is continuously evolving, with upcoming features that promise to enhance its capabilities and applications. Initiatives such as scaling solutions, enhanced interoperability with other blockchains, and further advancements in smart contract functionality signal a forward-thinking approach that addresses the dynamic nature of the blockchain landscape. As Cardano progresses, its unique features position it as a formidable contender in the competitive world of cryptocurrencies and decentralized finance, making it an exciting option for newcomers exploring the vast potential of blockchain technology.

Chapter 8: The Future of Cardano

Roadmap Overview

The roadmap overview for Cardano serves as a comprehensive guide to the platform's planned developments and milestones. Cardano is designed with a strong emphasis on scientific research and peer-reviewed methodologies, which is reflected in its carefully structured roadmap. This roadmap is divided into distinct eras, each with specific goals and features aimed at enhancing the platform's functionality and user experience. Understanding this roadmap is essential for anyone looking to navigate the Cardano ecosystem effectively.

The first era of the roadmap is the Byron era, which focused on the foundational aspects of Cardano. During this phase, the platform laid the groundwork for its blockchain and native cryptocurrency, ADA. The introduction of the Cardano wallet and the implementation of the Ouroboros consensus algorithm marked significant achievements. This era ensured that users had a secure and stable environment to transact and interact with the blockchain. For newcomers, grasping the importance of this foundational work is crucial, as it sets the stage for subsequent developments.

Following Byron, the Shelley era introduced decentralization to the Cardano network. This phase empowered users to run their own nodes and participate in the staking process, allowing for a more distributed network governance model. The shift towards decentralization is a key aspect of Cardano's mission, as it aligns with the broader goals of blockchain technology to enhance user control and eliminate single points of failure. New users should recognize how this era fosters community involvement and strengthens the network's resilience.

The Goguen era, which is currently underway, is focused on smart contract functionality. This is particularly relevant for those interested in Cardano's potential in decentralized finance (DeFi) and application development. With the introduction of smart contracts, developers can create complex decentralized applications (dApps) that leverage Cardano's unique features. Understanding this phase is vital for anyone looking to explore the development opportunities within the ecosystem and to grasp how Cardano aims to compete with other blockchain platforms in terms of functionality and usability.

Looking ahead, the roadmap continues to evolve with the upcoming Basho and Voltaire eras. Basho will enhance scalability and performance, while Voltaire will introduce a robust governance framework, enabling users to participate actively in decision-making processes. For beginners, this roadmap overview highlights the dynamic nature of Cardano and the commitment to continuous improvement. As the platform matures, it promises to deliver innovative features and applications that cater to the needs of its community, further solidifying its position in the rapidly changing blockchain landscape.

Upcoming Features and Enhancements

The Cardano ecosystem is continually evolving, with a robust roadmap that outlines upcoming features and enhancements aimed at improving user experience, increasing functionality, and expanding its capabilities. One of the most anticipated features is the introduction of improved smart contract functionality. Following the Alonzo upgrade, developers have been working diligently to enhance the Plutus smart contract platform, making it more user-friendly and efficient. This will allow newcomers to easily create and deploy their own decentralized applications (dApps), contributing to a vibrant development community and a wide array of use cases across various industries.

Another significant enhancement on the horizon is the further integration of interoperability features. Cardano aims to facilitate seamless interactions between different blockchain networks. By enabling cross-chain communication, Cardano will allow assets and information to flow more freely between ecosystems. This will not only enhance the user experience but also position Cardano as a vital player in the broader blockchain landscape, attracting users and developers from other platforms who seek greater flexibility and connectivity.

As decentralized finance (DeFi) continues to gain traction, Cardano is set to roll out a suite of DeFi applications that will empower users to engage in lending, borrowing, and yield farming directly on the platform. These applications will leverage Cardano's low transaction fees and high scalability, making DeFi more accessible to crypto newbies.

Additionally, the upcoming enhancements will include tools for liquidity providers and automated market makers, thus broadening the options available for users looking to participate in the DeFi space on Cardano.

Governance is another critical aspect of Cardano's evolution. The platform has been designed with a unique governance model that encourages community involvement in decision-making processes. Upcoming features will enhance this model, allowing ADA holders to have a more direct influence on the future direction of the network. This includes the potential for new voting mechanisms that simplify participation and ensure that a diverse range of voices are heard, fostering a truly decentralized governance structure.

Lastly, the future of Cardano is not only about technological advancements but also about community growth and education. Upcoming features will include enhanced educational resources aimed at newcomers to the ecosystem. These resources will help users understand the intricacies of Cardano, from staking to governance participation, ensuring that they can navigate the platform confidently. With each new feature and enhancement, Cardano reaffirms its commitment to creating an inclusive and user-friendly environment for everyone, from crypto novices to experienced developers.

Long-term Vision for Cardano

Long-term vision for Cardano revolves around its ambition to create a secure, scalable, and sustainable blockchain ecosystem that empowers individuals and businesses globally. The foundational philosophy of Cardano is rooted in a research-driven approach, which sets it apart from many other blockchain platforms. The goal is to develop a system that not only accommodates the growing needs of users but also fosters innovation in various sectors, including finance, education, and identity management. By leveraging a layered architecture, Cardano aims to provide a flexible platform that can evolve over time, adapting to new technological advancements and user requirements.

At the heart of Cardano's long-term vision is the commitment to decentralization. By employing a proof-of-stake (PoS) consensus mechanism, Cardano ensures that the network is not only secure but also energy-efficient compared to traditional proof-of-work systems. This approach allows ADA holders to participate in the network's operations, giving them a stake in its success and promoting community involvement. The long-term sustainability of Cardano's ecosystem relies on this decentralized governance model, which empowers users to influence the future direction of the platform through voting mechanisms.

Smart contracts play a crucial role in Cardano's future, as they enable developers to create decentralized applications (dApps) that can operate without intermediaries. The platform's unique scripting language, Plutus, is designed to facilitate the development of robust smart contracts, ensuring that they are secure and efficient. This focus on smart contracts opens up a myriad of possibilities for innovation, especially in the realms of decentralized finance (DeFi) and digital identity. Cardano envisions a future where businesses and individuals can seamlessly interact through dApps, enhancing efficiency and reducing costs across various industries.

Cardano's vision extends to fostering a vibrant ecosystem of decentralized finance applications. By providing the necessary infrastructure for DeFi, Cardano aims to democratize access to financial services, allowing anyone with an internet connection to participate. This includes services like lending, borrowing, and trading without the need for traditional banks or financial institutions. The long-term goal is to create a financial landscape that is more inclusive and accessible, empowering individuals in underserved regions to take control of their financial futures.

Ultimately, Cardano's roadmap is designed to evolve in response to the needs of its community and the broader market. The continuous development of features, alongside active participation from ADA stakeholders, is central to achieving this vision. As Cardano progresses, the focus will remain on ensuring security, scalability, and usability, enabling it to compete effectively with other blockchain platforms. The future of Cardano is not just about technological advancements but also about building a strong community that collaborates to shape the platform's trajectory, ensuring its relevance and success in the ever-evolving crypto landscape.

Chapter 9: Getting Started with Cardano

Setting Up a Wallet

Setting up a wallet is a crucial first step for anyone looking to engage with the Cardano ecosystem. A wallet allows users to store, send, and receive ADA, the native cryptocurrency of Cardano. There are various types of wallets available, including hot wallets, cold wallets, and hardware wallets. Hot wallets are connected to the internet, making them convenient for everyday transactions. Cold wallets, on the other hand, are offline and provide enhanced security for long-term storage. Hardware wallets combine the benefits of both by storing private keys securely while allowing easy access to funds when needed.

To get started, users should first choose the type of wallet that best suits their needs. For beginners, a hot wallet like Daedalus or Metamask is often recommended. Both wallets offer user-friendly interfaces and support for ADA. Daedalus is a full-node wallet that downloads the entire Cardano blockchain, providing greater security but requiring more storage space. Metamask, a lightweight wallet, operates as a browser extension or mobile app, making it ideal for those who prefer quick access and less resource consumption.

Once a wallet is selected, the next step is to create an account. This process typically involves downloading the wallet application, following the on-screen instructions, and setting up a secure password. Importantly, users will also be prompted to write down a recovery phrase, a set of words that serves as a backup in case the wallet is lost or access is compromised. It is crucial to store this recovery phrase in a safe place, as losing it can result in permanent loss of access to funds.

After setting up the wallet, users can proceed to fund it with ADA. This can be done by purchasing ADA from a cryptocurrency exchange, such as Binance or Coinbase, and then transferring it to the wallet address provided by the chosen wallet application. Each wallet will have a specific address format, and it's essential to double-check the address before initiating a transfer. Transactions on the Cardano blockchain are generally quick and affordable, making it easy to manage funds once the wallet is set up.

In addition to storing ADA, many wallets now offer features that enable users to participate in the Cardano ecosystem actively. For instance, some wallets allow staking, which lets users earn rewards by contributing to the network's security and operations. This feature aligns with Cardano's proof-of-stake consensus mechanism, providing an opportunity for users to engage in decentralized finance applications and governance processes. By setting up a wallet, users take the first step towards exploring the full potential of Cardano, paving the way for deeper involvement in its vibrant community.

Buying and Staking ADA

Buying ADA, the native cryptocurrency of the Cardano network, is a straightforward process that begins with selecting a cryptocurrency exchange. Popular exchanges such as Coinbase, Binance, and Kraken offer ADA trading pairs, allowing users to purchase ADA using fiat currencies like USD or EUR. Once you've chosen an exchange, you will need to create an account, complete the necessary identity verification, and deposit funds. After your account is funded, you can place a market or limit order to buy ADA. It is important to consider transaction fees and security measures, such as enabling two-factor authentication, to protect your investment.

After acquiring ADA, the next step is to store it securely. While you can keep your ADA on the exchange where you purchased it, this is generally not recommended due to potential security risks associated with exchanges. Instead, it is advisable to transfer your ADA to a personal wallet. There are various wallet options available, including hardware wallets like Ledger and Trezor, which provide enhanced security by storing your private keys offline. Alternatively, you can use software wallets, such as Daedalus, specifically designed for Cardano or Metamask, which allows you to hold many cryptocurrencies. These wallets allow you to manage your ADA and participate in staking.

Staking is one of the key features of Cardano's proof-of-stake consensus mechanism. By staking your ADA, you contribute to the network's security and operations while earning rewards in return. The staking process involves delegating your ADA to a stake pool, which is a group of ADA holders pooling their resources to increase their chances of being selected to validate transactions. To start staking, you can use your selected wallet to find a stake pool and delegate your ADA. It is essential to research different stake pools, considering factors such as performance, fees, and operator reputation, to maximize your staking rewards.

Rewards from staking are distributed approximately every five days, providing a consistent income stream for ADA holders. The amount of rewards you earn depends on the total amount of ADA you have staked and the performance of the stake pool you have chosen. It is also important to note that you can unstake your ADA at any time, giving you flexibility if you decide to change pools or sell your ADA. This feature encourages users to participate in the network while maintaining control over their assets.

Engaging in the Cardano ecosystem through buying and staking ADA not only provides potential financial benefits but also fosters a sense of community involvement. Cardano places a strong emphasis on governance, allowing stakeholders to participate in decision-making processes and vote on proposals. This democratic approach to network governance empowers users and encourages active participation in shaping the future of Cardano. As the ecosystem continues to grow and evolve, staying informed and actively participating in staking can help you maximize your engagement with Cardano and its innovative developments.

Resources for Continued Learning

As you embark on your journey to understand Cardano and its multifaceted ecosystem, a variety of resources are available to deepen your knowledge and keep you updated with the latest developments. Official documentation from the Cardano Foundation and IOHK serves as a foundational starting point. These resources provide comprehensive information about Cardano's technology, governance, and its unique approach to blockchain development. Engaging with the official documentation not only helps you grasp the underlying principles of Cardano but also keeps you informed about its ongoing evolution.

For those interested in smart contracts, various online platforms offer tutorials and courses specifically focused on Cardano's Plutus and Marlowe programming languages. Websites like Coursera and Udemy often feature courses tailored to beginners, allowing you to learn at your own pace. These platforms typically include hands-on projects that enhance your understanding of how to develop and deploy smart contracts within the Cardano ecosystem, making them valuable for aspiring developers and enthusiasts alike.

The role of Proof of Stake (PoS) in Cardano's ecosystem is another critical topic worth exploring. Numerous articles, research papers, and videos are available that explain how PoS differs from traditional Proof of Work (PoW) systems. Engaging with content from reputable blockchain analysts and thought leaders can provide insights into the advantages of PoS, particularly in terms of energy efficiency and scalability. Following reputable blockchain influencers on social media platforms can also provide continuous updates and discussions surrounding the benefits and challenges of PoS as implemented by Cardano.

Decentralized Finance (DeFi) applications are gaining traction, and Cardano is positioning itself as a significant player within this space. Online forums, such as Reddit and specialized Discord channels, are excellent places to engage with the community and learn about emerging DeFi projects on Cardano. These platforms facilitate discussions around various use cases, allowing newcomers to understand how Cardano's unique architecture supports DeFi initiatives. Participating in these discussions can also help you develop a network of like-minded individuals who share similar interests in blockchain technology.

Lastly, keeping an eye on Cardano's roadmap and upcoming features is essential for anyone invested in the ecosystem. The Cardano Foundation and IOHK regularly publish updates about new developments, partnerships, and technological advancements. Subscribing to their newsletters or following their official social media accounts ensures that you remain informed about the latest news. Additionally, attending webinars and community events can provide direct access to Cardano experts, allowing you to ask questions and engage in meaningful conversations about the future of Cardano. By utilizing these resources, you will be well-equipped to navigate the evolving landscape of Cardano and the broader blockchain ecosystem.